21st
Century
Junior
Library

# Hammers

*By Josh Gregory*

CHERRY LAKE PUBLISHING * ANN ARBOR, MICHIGAN

Published in the United States of America by Cherry Lake Publishing
Ann Arbor, Michigan
www.cherrylakepublishing.com

Content Adviser: Roger McGregor, Director, Hannibal Career and Technical Center, Hannibal, Missouri

Reading Adviser: Marla Conn, ReadAbility, Inc.

Photo Credits: Cover, ©Image Source/Alamy; page 4, ©bikeriderlondon/Shutterstock, Inc.; page 6, ©nednapa/Shutterstock, Inc.; page 8, ©Africa Studio/Shutterstock, Inc.; page 10, ©KAMONRAT/ Shutterstock, Inc.; page 12, ©Martin Green/Dreamstime.com; page 14, ©didden/Shutterstock, Inc.; page 16, ©ra2studio/Shutterstock, Inc.; page 18, ©John de la Bastide/Shutterstock, Inc.; page 20, ©suradech sribuanoy/Shutterstock, Inc.

**LIBRARY OF CONGRESS CATALOGING-IN-PUBLICATION DATA**
Gregory, Josh.
 Hammers/by Josh Gregory.
    pages cm.—(Basic tools) (21st century junior library)
 Audience: K to grade 3.
 Includes bibliographical references and index.
 ISBN 978-1-62431-168-0 (library binding)—ISBN 978-1-62431-300-4 (paperback)—
ISBN 978-1-62431-234-2 (e-book)
 1. Hammers—Juvenile literature. I. Title.
 TJ1201.H3G74 2013
 621.9'73—dc23                          2013004923

Cherry Lake Publishing would like to acknowledge the work of
The Partnership for 21st Century Skills.
Please visit www.p21.org for more information.

Printed in the United States of America
Corporate Graphics Inc.
July 2013
CLFA13

# CONTENTS

Hammers are used in all sorts of building projects.

# What Is a Hammer?

Have you ever looked inside a toolbox? If you have, you have probably seen a hammer. Hammers are very simple tools. They are used to hit things. People have used them for millions of years. They are just as useful now as they were then!

A hammer's shape and the materials used to make it affect how the hammer will be used.

The part of the hammer that hits things is the **head**. The part that a person holds is the handle. Sometimes the head and handle are all one piece. Other times, a head is attached to a separate handle piece.

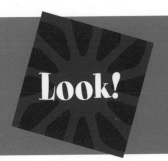

**Look!**

Do your parents own any hammers? Ask if you can look at them. How are the hammers alike? How are they different?

Some people prefer hammers with wood handles. Others prefer handles made of metal or other materials.

The very first hammers were made of rocks. Today's hammerheads are usually made of metal. Metal lasts longer than rock. It is also less likely to break. Most handles are made of metal or wood. Some handles have **rubber** around them. This keeps the hammer from slipping out of a worker's grip.

A hard, heavy hammer, such as this sledgehammer, is a great tool to use when tearing down walls.

# How Are Hammers Used?

Workers use hammers anytime they need to hit something. This means hammers are sometimes used to break things apart. Other times, they are used to build things.

Nails are sometimes used to attach one piece of wood to another.

Hammers are often used to pound nails into objects. Just like a hammer, a nail has a flat head. A nail also has a pointy end. Workers hit the hammerhead against the nailhead. This pushes the nail's pointy tip into a piece of wood.

**Make a Guess!**

Imagine you are making a rectangle out of four boards. Each board needs two nails to attach it to another board. How many nails do you need to make the rectangle?

Ball-peen hammers come in many sizes.

# Different Kinds of Hammers

Not all hammers are the same. Some work better than others for certain jobs. A ball-peen hammer is used to bend and shape pieces of metal. This hammer's head is round on one side. Ball-peen hammers are usually harder than other hammers. This keeps them from breaking when they hit pieces of metal.

People use mallets and sharp instruments called chisels to carve designs into stone and other materials.

Mallets have larger and lighter heads than most hammers. Mallet hammerheads are usually made out of wood, leather, or rubber. Workers use them to avoid damaging the objects they are hammering. People who make wooden furniture or toys use mallets. Wooden pieces are hammered into place using the mallet's soft head.

Sledgehammers are large and heavy. This helps them hit objects with a lot of force.

Sledgehammers are bigger and heavier than other hammers. Workers swing them to smash rocks or concrete into smaller pieces. They also use sledgehammers to knock down walls. Sometimes these hammers are used to drive **stakes** into the ground.

Hammers with a claw at one end are often
called claw hammers.

Some hammerheads have a **claw** at one end. The claw has a notch in it. The notch makes it easier to pull out nails. This makes the hammer very handy for **carpenters**.

Hammers have many different uses. What will you build with these amazing tools?

# GLOSSARY

**carpenters** (KAHR-puhn-turz) people who build or repair things made of wood

**claw** (KLAW) the part of a hammer that it used to pry up nails

**head** (HED) the end of a hammer that is used to hit things

**rubber** (RUHB-ur) a stretchy substance made from tree sap or produced in factories

**stakes** (STAYKS) posts with points at one end that can be driven into the ground to support something

# FIND OUT MORE

## BOOKS

Hanson, Anders. *Hammers.* Edina, MN: ABDO, 2010.

Nelson, Robin. *What Does a Hammer Do?* Minneapolis: Lerner, 2013.

## WEB SITES

### HowStuffWorks—Hammer

*http://home.howstuffworks.com /hammer.htm*
Read more about types of hammers and how they are used.

### The Hammer Museum

*www.hammermuseum.org*
Learn about a museum dedicated entirely to hammers.

# INDEX

## ABOUT THE AUTHOR

Josh Gregory writes and edits books for kids. He lives in Chicago, Illinois.